INSIDE YOUR BODY

ALL ABOUT BEE STINGS

MEGAN BORGERT-SPANIOL

Consulting Editor, Diane Craig, MA/Reading Specialist

Super Sandcastle

An Imprint of Abdo Publishing
abdopublishing.com

ABDOPUBLISHING.COM

Published by Abdo Publishing, a division of ABDO, PO Box
398166, Minneapolis, Minnesota 55439. Copyright © 2019
by Abdo Consulting Group, Inc. International copyrights
reserved in all countries. No part of this book may be
reproduced in any form without written permission from
the publisher. Super SandCastle™ is a trademark and logo
of Abdo Publishing.

Printed in the United States of America,
North Mankato, Minnesota
052018
092018

Design and Production: Mighty Media, Inc.
Editor: Jessie Alkire
Cover Photographs: iStockphoto; Shutterstock
Interior Photographs: iStockphoto; Shutterstock

Library of Congress Control Number: 2017961864

Publisher's Cataloging-in-Publication Data
Names: Borgert-Spaniol, Megan, author.
Title: All about bee stings / by Megan Borgert-Spaniol.
Description: Minneapolis, Minnesota : Abdo Publishing, 2019. |
    Series: Inside your body set 2
Identifiers: ISBN 9781532115790 (lib.bdg.) | ISBN 9781532156519
    (ebook)
Subjects: LCSH: Human body--Juvenile literature. | Bee stings--
    Juvenile literature. | Foreign-body reaction--Juvenile literature. |
    Bites and stings--Juvenile literature.
Classification: DDC 616.025--dc23

Super SandCastle™ books are created by a team of professional
educators, reading specialists, and content developers around five
essential components—phonemic awareness, phonics, vocabulary,
text comprehension, and fluency—to assist young readers as they
develop reading skills and strategies and increase their general
knowledge. All books are written, reviewed, and leveled for guided
reading, early reading intervention, and Accelerated Reader™
programs for use in shared, guided, and independent reading
and writing activities to support a balanced approach to literacy
instruction.

CONTENTS

YOUR BODY

YOU CAN GET STUNG ANYWHERE ON YOUR BODY

You're amazing! So is your body.

Most of the time your body works just fine. It lets you go to school, play with friends, and more. But sometimes you feel sick or part of you hurts.

Getting stung by a bee can hurt. But the pain usually doesn't last long. For some kids, bee stings cause serious problems. It is important to know what to do if a bee stings you!

5

ALL ABOUT BEE STINGS

Bees are insects with stingers. A bee's stinger is attached to a **venom** sac. If the bee stings you, its stinger goes into your skin. Venom travels through the stinger into your body. The venom causes **symptoms**.

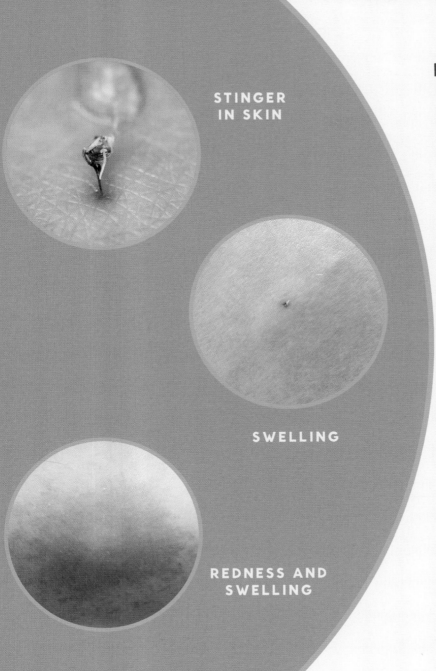

STINGER IN SKIN

SWELLING

REDNESS AND SWELLING

Honeybees can only sting once. This is because their stingers get stuck in skin. So, the honeybee loses its stinger after stinging.

Other bees can sting more than once. This is because they can pull their stingers out of skin. Then they fly away or sting again!

BEE-STUNG HAND

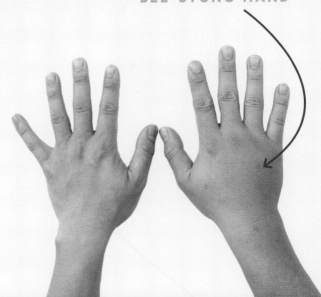

7

BEES
AND WASPS

It is easy to confuse bees with wasps. Wasps look a lot like bees. And they sting like bees too! Many people use the term *bee sting* to describe both bee and wasp stings.

You can identify a bee or wasp by how it looks. Watch for these insects and their nests in your yard!

HONEYBEE

Thin bodies, pointed rears, clear wings

Build wax hives above ground

Can only sting once

BUMBLEBEE

Fat and fuzzy bodies, rounded rears, dark wings

Often build nests on or under the ground

Can sting more than once

WASPS

BALD-FACED HORNET

Black with white markings, long and pointed bodies

Build papery nests in trees

Can sting more than once

YELLOW JACKET

Yellow with black stripes

Often build nests on the ground or in tree stumps

Can sting more than once

CAUSES

Bees and wasps do not always sting. They usually leave people alone. But these insects are likely to sting if they feel **threatened**.

Picnic Pests

Wasps like the same foods we do. That's why yellow jackets often show up at picnics. You might want to stop a wasp from sharing your food. But if you swat it, it might sting!

Swatting

This alarms bees and wasps. They sting to **defend** themselves.

Stepping on or disturbing a nest.

The insects will sting to defend their nests.

Standing close to a nest.

Wasps are protective of nests. They might feel **threatened** even if you're many feet away!

{ **FAST FACT** }

A bee or wasp's stinger is also used for laying eggs. Males do not have this body part. That means only female bees and wasps can sting!

SIGNS
AND SYMPTOMS

I f a bee or wasp stings you, you will know it! The insect's **venom** causes **symptoms** in your body.

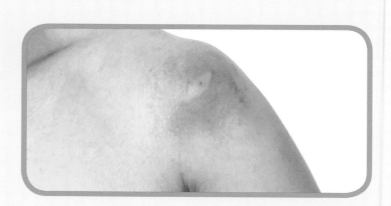

Common Symptoms

- Sharp, hot pain at the location of the sting

- Redness and swelling around the sting

- **Itching** around the sting

Most of the time, these symptoms are mild. They often go away within a day.

If you are stung by many bees, your **symptoms** may be different. The increased **venom** can make you feel sick. You should see a doctor right away if you have these symptoms.

VOMITING
OR DIARRHEA

HEADACHE

FEVER

DIZZINESS
OR FAINTING

TREATMENT

If you get a bee sting, tell an adult right away. He or she can watch your **symptoms**. Bee stings can usually be treated at home.

See Ya, Stinger

You can remove a stinger with your fingernails. You can also use a credit card or paper to scrape it off your skin.

REMOVE THE STINGER FROM YOUR SKIN. THEN WASH THE STING WITH SOAP AND WATER.

PLACE AN ICE PACK OVER THE STING TO RELIEVE PAIN AND SWELLING.

APPLY CALAMINE LOTION TO THE STING. THIS REDUCES REDNESS, ITCHING, AND SWELLING.

AVOID SCRATCHING. THIS WILL MAKE THE ITCHING WORSE! IT ALSO MIGHT CAUSE AN INFECTION.

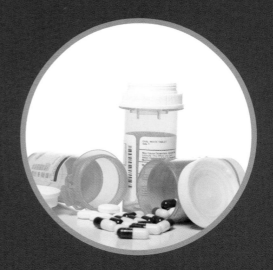

If the pain is bad, some medicines can help.

- Pain relievers help ease discomfort.

- Antihistamines relieve **itching** and swelling.

ALLERGIES

Some people are **allergic** to bee **venom**. This means their bodies work extra hard to fight the venom. To do this, their bodies release histamines.

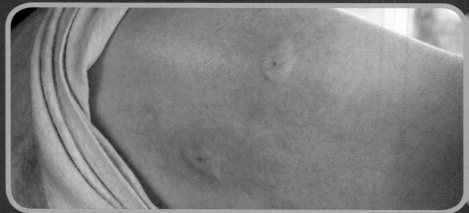

HISTAMINES
(*HIS-tah-meenz*)

chemicals released during an allergic **reaction**

Histamines cause **symptoms**. These symptoms are usually stronger than regular bee sting symptoms. This often means greater swelling and redness.

Allergic reactions don't usually occur the first time you get stung. Notice if your symptoms get stronger the next time you are stung. This may mean you have an allergy.

EMERGENCY!

If you are **allergic** to bee **venom**, a sting can be very harmful. It might cause a severe allergic **reaction**. These **symptoms** occur soon after the bee stings.

DIZZINESS OR FAINTING

WHEEZING

DIFFICULTY SWALLOWING OR BREATHING

RAPID HEARTBEAT

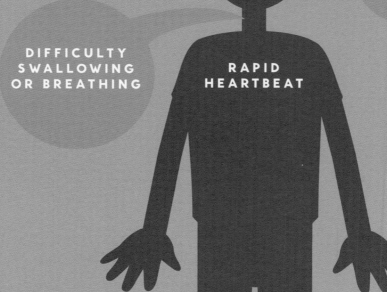

SWOLLEN LIPS, TONGUE, OR THROAT

VOMITING OR DIARRHEA

911

EMERGENCY CALL

These **symptoms** need immediate medical attention. Call 9-1-1 or go to an emergency room right away!

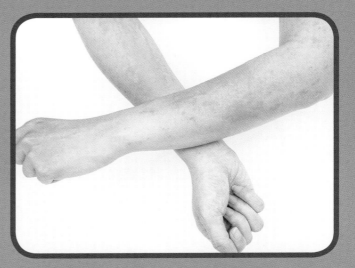

HIVES

GOING TO THE
DOCTOR

Bee stings do not commonly cause severe **reactions**. But there are other reasons you might need medical attention after being stung.

When to See a Doctor

You were stung near or inside your mouth

Your **symptoms** last for a few days

You were stung multiple times

Your symptoms are stronger than the last time you were stung

The site of the sting looks **infected**

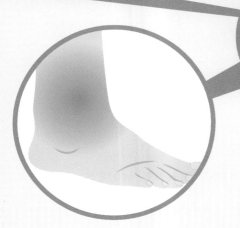

Is it Infected?

Look out for signs of an infected bee sting. These include increased redness, warmth, and **pus**.

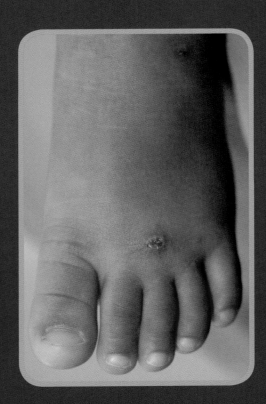

PREVENTION

Being careful can help prevent a bee sting. While outdoors, take these steps to avoid bees and their stingers!

ALWAYS WEAR SHOES OUTSIDE.

WATCH FOR BEE AND WASP NESTS. KEEP YOUR DISTANCE!

COVER FOOD AND DRINKS WHEN POSSIBLE. WASPS LIKE TO CRAWL INTO OPEN BOTTLES AND CANS.

AVOID WEARING BRIGHT CLOTHING
AND SCENTED LOTIONS OR
PERFUMES THAT ATTRACT INSECTS.

STAY CALM IF A BEE OR WASP
COMES NEAR YOU. SLOWLY WALK
AWAY INSTEAD OF SWATTING AT IT.

COVER YOUR MOUTH AND NOSE
IF THERE ARE INSECTS FLYING
AROUND YOU.

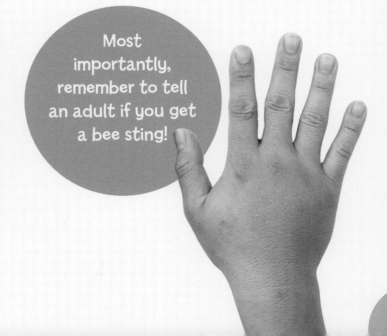

Most importantly, remember to tell an adult if you get a bee sting!

ALLERGY - a sickness caused by touching, breathing, or eating certain things. Something related to an allergy is called allergic.

DEFEND - to protect from harm or attack.

INFECTION - an unhealthy condition caused by bacteria or other germs. If something has an infection, it is infected.

ITCHING - feeling irritated or bothersome.

PUS - a thick, yellowish substance the body produces when it has an infection.

REACTION - a response to a stimulus.

SYMPTOM - a noticeable change in the normal working of the body.

THREATENED - frightened by something.

VENOM - a poison made by some animals and insects. It usually enters a victim through a bite or a sting.

GLOSSARY